MIND, BODY, & Soul

A Self-Care Coloring Book for Black Women

Oludara Adeeyo
Author of *Self-Care for Black Women*

Illustrated by Tess Armstrong

ADAMS MEDIA
NEW YORK LONDON TORONTO SYDNEY NEW DELHI

T0273484

Adams Media
An Imprint of Simon & Schuster, Inc.
100 Technology Center Drive
Stoughton, Massachusetts 02072

First Adams Media trade paperback edition January 2024

ADAMS MEDIA and colophon are registered trademarks of Simon & Schuster, Inc.

Simon & Schuster: Celebrating 100 Years of Publishing in 2024

For information about special discounts for bulk purchases, please contact Simon & Schuster Special Sales at 1-866-506-1949 or business@simonandschuster.com.

The Simon & Schuster Speakers Bureau can bring authors to your live event. For more information or to book an event, contact the Simon & Schuster Speakers Bureau at 1-866-248-3049 or visit our website at www.simonspeakers.com.

Interior design by Erin Alexander
Illustrations by Tess Armstrong

Manufactured in the United States of America

10 9 8 7 6 5 4 3

ISBN 978-1-5072-2162-4

Dedication

Dedicated to Black women who have decided to put themselves first. May this coloring book bring you peace—and encourage you to continue to choose yourself.

Acknowledgments

Thank you to everyone who has supported my first two books: *Self-Care for Black Women* and *Affirmations for Black Women: A Journal*. It has been quite a journey, and the next trip takes us to *Mind, Body, & Soul: A Self-Care Coloring Book for Black Women*. I hope you enjoy it. To Tess Armstrong, thank you for bringing my affirmations to life with your artwork. This is our third book together, and I love getting to see my words depicted in your fantasy world. And a special thanks to everyone at Adams Media and Simon & Schuster who worked on this project. Your continued care with this subject matter is appreciated. Thank you.

Contents

Introduction

It's time for a wellness check. When was the last time you practiced self-care? Have you been prioritizing your well-being? Hopefully you answered these questions with recently and yes. If not, that's okay. I got you. In *Mind, Body, & Soul: A Self-Care Coloring Book for Black Women*, you will get the chance to create space for yourself to manifest, validate, and recognize your power and worth. Your self-confidence is about to get a boost, girl.

Self-care is a journey. It's not only preventative care for your overall health, but also your personal path to healing your mind, body, and soul. Creative expression is a great way to support these goals, and coloring can help you unwind your mind, relax your nervous system, and reconnect with your inner being. Throughout *Mind, Body, & Soul: A Self-Care Coloring Book for Black Women*, you'll find thirty-five illustrations paired with powerful affirmations—positive statements that transform your living experience and change the way you think. As you color, you will feel seen and empowered by these words and images.

Choosing to put yourself first is a radical act for Black women. The world is tough on us. As Black women, we are often asked by society to dismiss and suppress our hardships. This can have a negative impact on our mental, physical, and spiritual health. Because of this, we must be proactive about preserving our peace through self-care activities like coloring. So grab your colored pencils, markers, or crayons, and enjoy this special self-care time. You deserve it.

✧ ✦ ✧

I deserve to experience Black girl joy.

✧

I no longer talk bad about myself.

✧

I will break generational curses.

✧ ✦ ✧

I deserve to celebrate myself whenever I want.

✦ ◇ ✦

Asking others for help is a power move.

✧ ◇ ◇

I am gentle with myself through life's transitions.

Moving through life with ease is my ancestral right.

It is okay to grieve at my own pace.

✦

I can connect to the parts of my family that bring me joy.

I recognize rest as a form of self-love.

✦ ✧ ✦

I am open to all streams of income.

My work ethic is more than enough.

✦

I release the things I cannot change.

✧

Maintaining my mental health is a priority.

✧

I accept the shape of my body.

✧

Choosing to start over does not mean I have failed.

✧ ✧ ✧

I trust that I will reach all of my desired goals.

✧

I can say no without an explanation.

I pour into myself before I pour into others.

✧

I take time to explore my purpose.

I don't have to justify my need for rest.

My failures are not a reflection of my worth.

My fears will not stop me from pursuing my dreams.

I understand that exercise helps me to reconnect with myself.

✧

I listen to my inner child's needs to help me heal.

✦ ✦ ✦

My hair is beautiful and unique.

I trust that good things are coming my way.

✦

I recognize rejection as redirection and protection.

✧ ✧ ✧

I attract loving and supportive relationships.

My life is not defined by my trauma.

I understand the power of a good night's rest.

I trust that my body knows what I need.

I give myself permission to create boundaries with others.

✧

I don't allow my negative thoughts to consume me.

✧

I let go of people-pleasing by focusing on myself.

Author photo by Adán S. Velásquez Méndez

About the Author

Oludara Adeeyo is a mental health therapist and the author of *Self-Care for Black Women* and *Affirmations for Black Women: A Journal.* She is passionate about helping people, especially Black women, improve their overall wellness. Before becoming a licensed clinical social worker, Oludara worked as a writer and editor. She has been an associate web editor at *Cosmopolitan* and the managing editor at *XXL.* Oludara is based out of Los Angeles. Follow her on social media to keep up with her latest work at @oludaraadeeyo.

Illustrator photo by Rhys Mavis

About the Illustrator

Tess Armstrong is a graphic designer and freelance illustrator with a BS in graphic design from the Art Institute of California, San Diego. Determined to represent more Black women and women of color, Tess incorporates strong female characters in her work, illuminated through whimsical scenes of sirens, fairies, and more in colorful paintings, murals, and digital illustrations. This is her third work with Oludara Adeeyo. Her past works include *Self-Care for Black Women* and *Affirmations for Black Women: A Journal*. Follow her world of fantasy on *Instagram* at @tessarmstrongart.

Includes 150 self-care exercises designed specifically for Black women

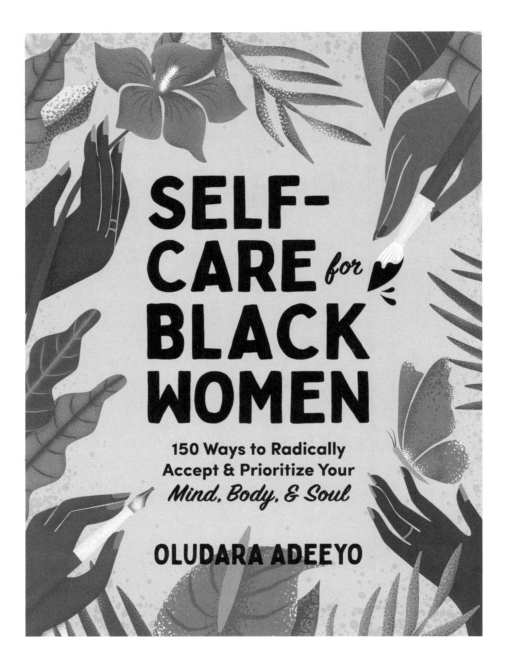

SELF-CARE for BLACK WOMEN

150 Ways to Radically Accept & Prioritize Your *Mind, Body, & Soul*

OLUDARA ADEEYO

Pick up or download your copy today!

adamsmedia
An Imprint of Simon & Schuster
A Paramount Company